PRESENTED TO

. . . .

PRESENTED BY

. . . .

DATE

. . . .

God Cares for You and You're Safely in His Hands
Copyright © 2017 by DaySpring
Print ISBN 978-1-68408-117-2

Manuscript written by Rebecca Currington in association with Snapdragon Editorial Group℠, Tulsa, Oklahoma.

Published by:

DaySpring

P.O. Box 1010
Siloam Springs, AR 72761
dayspring.com

God Cares for you

AND YOU'RE SAFELY IN HIS HANDS

*If God cares
so wonderfully
for flowers
that are here today
and gone tomorrow,
won't He more surely
care for you?*

MATTHEW 6:30 TLB

Is anyone crying
for help?
GOD is listening,
ready to rescue you.

PSALM 34:17 THE MESSAGE

Introduction

You're holding this book in your hand, so maybe you're wondering...***Does God know what's going on in my life? Does He care that I'm hurting? How involved is God with the daily details of my life anyway?*** We pray that as you read through these pages, that question will be resolved in your heart and mind.

Of course, it's difficult for any of us to understand why the Great Creator—the one who set the stars in the sky and put the oceans in place, the one who arranged the planets and keeps them spinning in perfect orbits—would care about us. But the Bible tells us that He knows us intimately and cares about us deeply. The whole purpose of this book is to convey to you the reality of God's love for you and His longing to help you. He knows your every need!

He knows—but we don't. That's why, for the purposes of this book, we've chosen needs that are common to all of us and provided an encouraging message with a scripture to help you better understand God's stated intention for you. Each entry ends with a prayer to begin a dialogue between you and the Lover of your soul, the good heavenly Father, your Creator and God.

You may be at the top of your game or the lowest point in your life. Wherever you are, God is there. He knows... and He cares!

TABLE OF CONTENTS

God Knows...

God Knows...
You feel like you're all alone
...and He cares.

TURN TO ME AND BE GRACIOUS TO ME,
FOR I AM LONELY.
PSALM 25:16 NASB

That painful sense of loneliness you're feeling right now—it's a gift from God. It's true! Meaningful interaction with others is a basic human need, imbedded in our hearts by the Creator Himself. Without it, we would lack the desire to work together and take care of each other.

This means that God not only understands what you're feeling, but He is also hoping you will act on it in the way He, your Creator, intended. Instead of interpreting this painful aspect of your life as a negative, think of it as God encouraging you to become the answer to someone else's loneliness as well as your own.

When you go out of your way to offer an encouraging word or engage in an act of unsolicited kindness, you almost always find there are people all around you—people who need you as much as you need them. If you don't find these people on the first try, keep looking. Ask God to send them across your path. Slowly but surely, you will find their familiar faces are replacing what once was just a painful longing.

Father God, lead me to those who,

like me, are lonely and longing

for satisfying friendship.

I promise to keep reaching out

and ask that You would encourage

those who need my friendship to respond.

Thank You for banishing my

loneliness and opening up a

whole new world for me.

Amen.

God Knows...
You need help
...and He cares.

WHERE DOES MY HELP COME FROM? MY HELP COMES
FROM THE LORD WHO MADE HEAVEN AND EARTH.
PSALM 121:1-2 NCV

You've done everything you know to do, and still you can't find a way out of your present situation. Now you're wondering if God has even noticed, and if He knows, does He care? Of course He does!

There are times in each of our lives when it seems that every friend has vanished and every pathway has been blocked. All those surefire solutions we've banked on in the past have failed. But when we are surrounded by mountains on every side, God has invited us to call on Him, the one who has all the resources of the universe with which to help us. And His help comes without judgment, without strings attached, and without payback with interest. God's help isn't free, but the cost has been already been paid. And it's offered with more love than we could ever know.

So look up. Open your eyes and your heart to God. Acknowledge your need, and ask for His help. He has promised to answer as soon as you ask!

Dear Father, as I look up to You,
my heart is filled with renewed hope.
Thank You for helping me
without asking for anything in return.
As I move forward,
may my eyes stay focused
on Your goodness and
Your great love for me.
Amen.

God Knows...
You long to laugh out loud
...and He cares.

THE LORD LAUGHS AT THE WICKED FOR HE SEES THAT HIS DAY IS COMING.
PSALM 37:13 ESV

When was the last time you laughed so hard your eyes watered, your whole body shook, and you had trouble catching your breath? Do you remember? Sure, it's hard to laugh when there are so many reasons to feel discouraged, disillusioned, and heartsick. What you need is a God's-eye view.

Imagine yourself looking down from a vantage point high up on the highest mountain. We'll call this your "high corner." Get comfortable, relax, and then take a peek. Those evil giants look like puny little bugs from up here, don't they? Go ahead and have a good laugh at them running in circles.

God has a plan, and He's working it out in our lives and in our world. Yes, He cries when He sees the suffering, but He laughs at those who think they can inflict suffering on others without having to answer for it. So allow yourself a good laugh at the absurdity of those who deride you and say you are nothing. Laugh until your sides ache. And then thank God for His love and care.

Dear Father,

things look so different

from up here on my "high corner."

Thank You for caring about me

and helping me see

the enemies of my soul with new eyes.

Now I know I can replace my fear

with laughter as I delight in

Your great love for me.

Amen.

God Knows...
You lack confidence
...and He cares.

**YOU ARE MY HOPE, LORD GOD,
MY CONFIDENCE FROM MY YOUTH.**
PSALM 71:5 HCSB

Confidence begins with a positive attitude, the assurance that you can meet the challenges of each new day. If you are a God-follower, you have reason to be supremely confident because He holds the future in His hands.

Nothing surprises God or catches Him off guard because He knows everything—your past, your present, and even your future. He is able to see the rocky path ahead and make a way for you to go through it. His foreknowledge enables Him to see every trial, every hardship, every heartbreak, and every disappointment. He is always prepared to provide exactly what you need.

Walking through life with God doesn't mean you will never encounter obstacles or hardships. It doesn't mean you will sail through every circumstance or situation with a smile on your face. What it means is that you will never have to go through those difficulties alone. The One who knows all and sees all will be standing right by your side showing you the way. That should give you all the confidence you could ever need.

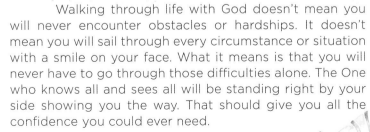

Heavenly Father,

thank You for always standing by me.

I am confident

that You will show me the way

around every obstacle

and provide the grace

to tackle every challenge.

Amen.

God Knows...
You long for lasting love
...and He cares.

**THE LOVING-KINDNESS OF THE LORD
IS FROM EVERLASTING TO EVERLASTING
TO THOSE WHO REVERENCE HIM.**
PSALM 103:17 TLB

Isn't it too bad love doesn't come with a guarantee? We could risk sharing our hearts without the fear of rejection, betrayal, or deceit. We could be certain that the words and actions of those who say they love us would always be true and genuine. Unfortunately, we will never receive love with a guarantee from another person. Human beings are barely capable of love for a lifetime, let alone love that lasts forever.

God's love, however, comes complete with an eternal guarantee—a guarantee He has put down in writing. While human beings may have good intentions, only God has the ability to carry out His intentions without exception. He knows us completely and accepts us unconditionally, and His love for us never ends.

You could say God has given us a proposal. How will you answer Him? Will you say, "Yes, yes," and give Him your heart? Or will you draw back? God doesn't ask you for a guarantee. He knows you aren't able to give Him one. He just asks you to accept His.

Father God, thank You for
Your pure and everlasting love for me.
My answer is, "Yes, yes."
I give my heart to You,
thankful that You love me
and see me with the unflinching eyes
of a loving father.
Amen.

God Knows...
You need to be comforted
...and He cares.

**GOD IS THE FATHER WHO IS FULL OF MERCY
AND ALL COMFORT.**
2 CORINTHIANS 1:3 NCV

If you're a parent, you know it's tough to watch your child struggle. But struggle is part of life. We allow our children to fall down and get back up so they can learn how to survive in this world.

In much the same way, God is our father—our parent. He could eliminate all that struggle and just supernaturally scoot us along to the finish line. But He knows the struggle is essential. All that falling down and getting back up teaches us to be strong and persevering. It helps us grow up in our faith.

Yes, God is a good father, a purposeful, caring father. And like all good parents, He is always near, always watching, ready to help us tenderly to our feet. Then He gently urges us forward. Whatever you are going through, reach out to Him. He will not chide or berate. Instead He will cover you with His love, encouragement, and comfort.

Dear Father
of all comfort,
thank You for helping me
grow up in my faith.
Thank You for also staying near
to comfort and encourage me up
when I fall.
Amen.

God Knows...
You've lost a loved one
...and He cares.

MY HEART IS SORE PAINED WITHIN ME:
AND THE TERRORS OF DEATH ARE FALLEN UPON ME.
PSALM 55:4 KJV

The realization bears down on you like a leaden cloud. As each day passes, more and more places seem empty without that special face to greet you, the familiar voice on the phone. With a broken heart, you have come to acknowledge the reality of death.

Yet just as present with you is the reality of God's love and concern for you. His love alone has the power to lift the cloud of sorrow and shine the soft light of comfort and consolation to your deepest, darkest grief. Especially during this hour of sorrow and uncertainty, let God reveal His plans for you page by page. You may not be able to imagine anything good coming out of your loss, but remember who has written your life's story—One who cares about everything that happens to you.

Take comfort in sweet memories. Fill your heart with thanksgiving for all that your loved one meant to you. Most of all, put your trust in God. The reality of His love endures forever.

Lord of Life, fill my heart
with the reality of Your love.
Help me through the coming days and months
as I cope with my loss,
and grant me the strength and courage
to one day enter a new chapter of my life
with assurance and hope.

Amen.

God Knows...
You long to be forgiven
...and He cares.

**THROUGH HIM FORGIVENESS OF SINS
IS PROCLAIMED TO YOU.**
ACTS 13:38 NASB

If you break your favorite vase, no amount of glue will fix it completely. The crack may be difficult to see, but it will always be there. Our relationship with God is also broken. There have been many human attempts to put the pieces back together, but relationship with a holy God can't be mended—only replaced by something new. Fortunately for us, God has made a way for us to enter into a new relationship with Him—forgiveness through His Son, Jesus.

All we need do to receive God's forgiveness is ask for it. It's an act couched in simplicity, but it isn't necessarily easy. Our old sin nature doesn't want to acknowledge our deep need for God. Pride lifts its ugly head, and the invitation goes unanswered.

God is patient, however. As soon as you reach up to Him, His hand is extended down to you. God loves you. He greatly desires to walk in daily fellowship with you. Maybe you've already accepted His offer. If not, will you let Him replace your old, broken relationship with a brand new one?

Thank You, Lord,
for forgiveness and a beautiful,
new relationship with You.
I acknowledge my need for You
and receive Your forgiveness.
Amen.

God Knows...
You need guidance
...and He cares.

If you were to find yourself lost in the forest, chances are intuition alone wouldn't be enough to lead you to safety. What you would need is a knowledgeable, trustworthy guide—someone who has intimate knowledge of the terrain.

When it comes to life, God is just such a guide. He knows the journey that lies ahead of you. He knows where each decision you make will lead. When you come to a crossroad and don't know which way to turn, all you need to do is ask Him to point you in the right direction. He's already given you the Bible as your map and truth as your compass. Add to that God's Spirit as your guide, and you will be able to make it through any wilderness, from embarking on a new career to providing direction for your children.

Of course, you are always free to find your own way. God has gone to great lengths to ensure your freedom to do just that. He has promised, however, to provide His guidance without hesitation whenever you ask for it.

Father, my head is swimming
with possibilities, but I need You
to show me the way.
Even if I were able to find my own path,
I would almost certainly
miss important side trips along the way.
Thank You for making Your guidance
available to me.
Amen.

God Knows...
You've lost your sense of expectation
...and He cares.

MY SOUL, WAIT SILENTLY FOR GOD ALONE,
FOR MY EXPECTATION IS FROM HIM.
PSALM 62:5 NKJV

A mother and father waiting for the birth of their child are said to be "expecting." This special time overshadows everything else in their lives. As the baby grows, so does their sense of excitement and anticipation. Average days take on a deeper significance as they wait for that day of jubilation when their child finally arrives.

God's presence in our lives gives us reason to live a life of expectation as well. We should wake each morning eager to see what the day will bring, how God's goodness will play out for us. Without Him, we have only the promise that our bodies will become older and weaker. But with Him, life becomes "eternal life" with all His joyous promises spread out before us.

If you are a God follower, you have every reason to expect to see good things. Wait for them, anticipate them, prepare for them. Keep your eyes open. Your days are certain to take on deeper significance as you await that day of jubilation when you finally see your God face to face.

Father God, I choose to wait
with great expectation for Your
good promises to be fulfilled in my life,
the greatest of which is the gift of an eternity
spent in Your presence.

Amen.

God cares for you,
so turn all your
worries over
to him.

1 PETER 5:7 CEV

God Knows...
You need to control your thoughts
...and He cares.

WHEN MY ANXIOUS THOUGHTS MULTIPLY WITHIN ME,
YOUR CONSOLATIONS DELIGHT MY SOUL.
PSALM 94:19 NASB

There are few things as unsettling as being harassed by restless thoughts or unanswered questions. Your mind seems to whirl out of control, pulling you helplessly through endless mental dialogues and countless "what ifs." It's a difficult way to live, upsetting your equilibrium as well as derailing your inner joy and peace.

God cares about those things that keep you awake at night. We read in Scripture that God knows what you need and has a solution in process before you even ask. But unless you know and believe that, you're left thinking you have to work through every situation on your own. You will find relief from those troubling thoughts only when you are able to acknowledge that God has better solutions for your problems than you could ever come up with, and He is fully committed to setting those solutions in motion.

The next time you find yourself plagued by runaway thoughts, invite your heavenly Father to take charge. He will give you insight and help you separate the real from the imagined. Soon you will be back on track, ready to focus productively and creatively on the matters at hand..

Father in heaven,

I do believe that You care

and You've prepared a solution

for every problem in my life.

Forgive me for thinking

that somehow I could

come up with a better way on my own.

Calm my unbridled thoughts,

and restore joy and peace to my mind.

Amen.

God Knows...
You're tired of doing without
...and He cares.

THE POOR CAN RUN TO YOU BECAUSE YOU ARE
A FORTRESS IN TIMES OF TROUBLE.
PSALM 9:9 CEV

Being without the things you need, especially in a nation spilling over with affluence, is not easy to accept. You could become obsessed with socio-economic limitations, or you could stage a protest, carry a sign, and march on government offices. But what would that really accomplish? On the other hand, God can help you tackle the problem of need in your life.

When you go to God with your questions and challenges, He has promised to help you find viable, real-time solutions. He may use available resources—government programs, private charities, or generous people—but He certainly isn't limited to them. God always looks inward first. He wants to ensure long-term relief by dispelling a myriad of lies that you may have accepted as truth. He wants you free from spoilers like guilt concerning unwise choices, damage to your self-worth, and misperceptions about the nature of God's will, to name just a few.

God cares about your frustration and need. Let Him lift the constraints that have been keeping you down. Then you will be able to access His goodness, walk through doors of opportunity, and even receive the miracle of provision He has prepared for you.

Dear Lord,
thank You for pulling me back
from the allure of quick fixes
and turning my eyes toward You,
the one who loves me
and has made provision for my needs.
I want to have all my needs met
physically and spiritually.
Amen.

God Knows...
You find it difficult to pray
...and He cares.

Prayer can feel intimidating when you get all caught up in using the right words and conveying the proper message. But prayer isn't a speech; it's simple conversation that just happens to be with God. At times, it doesn't even require words. Tears, sighs, your expressions, and even silence are ways that you might communicate with your heavenly Father.

The Bible tells us that we are always in God's presence. He knows our every thought before we even put it into words. The verbal element in prayer is really meant to initiate faith and generate trust in our own hearts and minds.

Try thinking of God as the King of kings and yourself as the King's beloved child. He has given you freedom to spend time with Him whenever you like, and He has invited you to relax in His presence and speak your mind freely. So when you wake in the morning and before you go to sleep at night, have a conversation with your Father, the King. Tell Him what's on your mind, ask for His wise counsel, and share your dreams. If you like, you can even use words!

Father God,

thank You for inviting me

into Your presence and hearing

the cry of my heart

even before the words are spoken.

Help me as I learn to enter

into conversation with You,

relax in Your presence,

and listen for Your reply.

Amen.

God Knows...
You work too hard
...and He cares.

WHATEVER YOU DO, DO IT HEARTILY,
AS TO THE LORD AND NOT TO MEN
COLOSSIANS 3:23 NKJV

There's nothing wrong with hard work. Many people thrive on it. What may be making it seem too hard is how you view the work itself. If you see it as unproductive, beneath you, unappreciated, or misaligned with your talents and skills, you will almost certainly feel the weight of it more acutely.

Regardless of how many hours you work or what kind of boss you might have, dedicating your work effort to the Lord can make all the difference. For example, begin to focus on how your work makes a positive impact on the world around you. Even if you work digging postholes or alone in a dusty back room, you can still see yourself doing that job for the Lord and trust Him to give your hard work value and permanence. What if God is grooming you for an opportunity you haven't even imagined? Would that change how you do your job?

It doesn't matter if your job is to manage the White House or a drive-thru window. Put your whole heart into what you do. God sees, He cares, and He will use what you do for His great purposes.

Dear Lord,

I feel tired and frustrated

concerning the work I do.

Open up a new opportunity for me

or help me see my current job

as Your will for me at present.

Help me see each task I perform

as a service to You and a way to express my love

and gratitude.

Amen.

God Knows...

You aren't sure He's real
...and He cares.

GOD IS NOT A MAN, THAT HE SHOULD LIE, NOR A SON OF MAN, THAT HE SHOULD REPENT.
NUMBERS 23:19 NKJV

You may have been encouraged to believe some unbelievable things when you were a child, like the tooth fairy exchanges teeth for cash or Santa Claus perches his sleigh on the roof of your house to personally deliver your Christmas gifts. Now you know those things were fairy tales, and you wonder if God's presence in your life is also just a pretend story.

You can be certain that God is no fairy tale. Study the Bible, and read the promises God has put there for you. Then put Him to the test. God doesn't mind proving Himself to you. Start with your most desperate need, claim His promise, and watch Him keep it in a personal and satisfying way.

God is so much more than myth and legend. He is truly the Creator of the universe and the Savior of our souls. He doesn't need to lie or embellish or fabricate the story of His birth and death. It's all true; it always has been, and it always will be. The greatest witness of that truth is in our hearts.

Dear God,

I want to believe,

so I've decided to put You to the test.

If You're real,

let me see Your hand in my life,

let me feel Your presence in my soul,

and let me hear Your voice

speaking to my heart.

Amen.

God Knows...
You feel hopeless
...and He cares.

I REJOICE AND AM GLAD. EVEN MY BODY HAS HOPE.
PSALM 16:9 NCV

You could say that hope is like a life preserver in the midst of a storm at sea. Without it, your head would slip below the waves of discouragement and despair. You don't just need hope. You won't survive without it.

Hope disappears when we depend too much on people and things that fail us and leave us stranded on the "island of hopeless." It's even risky to place our hope in our national pride or concepts like the inherent goodness of humankind. Everybody and everything fails eventually—but not God. Place your hope in Him, and you will never find yourself feeling hopeless again.

When storm clouds gather on the horizon or a torrential downpour of calamity has caught you by surprise, hold fast to your hope in God. Read and meditate on His promises in the Bible. Then learn to trust Him with one situation at a time. Soon your heart will be filled with hope, and the storm clouds will no longer signal doom. Instead they will represent opportunities to place your hope again and again in your great and loving God.

Dear Lord,

I've already discovered

that there's no hope in this world for me.

Show me that hope can grow

and thrive in my heart

as I place all I have

in Your mighty hands.

Amen.

God Knows...
You wonder what life is about
...and He cares.

THERE'S NOTHING BETTER TO DO THAN GO AHEAD
AND...GET THE MOST WE CAN OUT OF LIFE.
IT'S GOD'S GIFT.
ECCLESIASTES 3:9 THE MESSAGE

You've probably heard someone respond to a disappointing outcome by saying, "That's life." Makes it sound like life is something to be endured rather than lived, doesn't it? On the other hand, you've probably heard someone say, "Life is beautiful," and you wonder if that person has a taxing job like you do, bills to pay, and a family to take care of. In fact, life consists of both of these perspectives and much more.

Life is God's gift, but He hasn't left you to navigate all its wonders and difficulties on your own. He's given you an instruction manual to go with it. The commandments and principles laid out in the Bible are not intended to condemn you or send you chasing after some unattainable standard. God designed them to help you get the most out of life—one moment, hour, and day at a time.

In addition to the precious gift of life He's given you and the instruction manual that goes with it, God has promised to walk through each new day with you. Together you will discover what life is all about.

Father God,

thank You for giving me life.

Even when I am going

through difficult times,

I realize the wonder of being alive.

Help me as I apply the principles

in the Bible to the issues in my life.

Amen.

God Knows...
You're in need of mercy
...and He cares.

GOD'S MERCY IS SO ABUNDANT,
AND HIS LOVE FOR US IS SO GREAT.
EPHESIANS 2:4 GNT

Long before you were born, God knew and loved the person you would one day be and initiated a generous and merciful plan to redeem your life. He knew you would struggle against sin and ultimately lose, so He conquered sin and canceled its judgment. Now His mercy is available to you every day.

If you feel you have failed God, you have a lot of company. We've all gone astray and disappointed our Creator. We all need His mercy to free us from guilt and condemnation. Fortunately, His mercy and grace are available to all, without regard for who we are or what we've done. God does have one condition, however. He asks that His gift of mercy be passed on to those who fail us. He expects us to give as freely as we have received.

Why linger in a prison of sin and shame when You have been given the key to freedom and a new beginning? Throw yourself on God's mercy, and immerse yourself in His love and grace. Receive what He provided for you long before you were even born.

Dear Father God,

I need Your mercy.

I know I've failed You,

I've failed myself,

and I've failed everyone who cares for me.

You've opened the door for me.

Give me the courage to walk through it.

Amen.

God Knows...
You have a problem with pride
...and He cares.

DO NOT LET SELFISHNESS OR PRIDE BE YOUR GUIDE.
PHILIPPIANS 2:3 NCV

We live in a culture that urges us to demand our rights, push forward our agendas, and celebrate ourselves. No wonder humility doesn't sell well. Its premise is that we should waive our rights and take a lower place than is our due. It is, however, the example Jesus left for us when He walked here on earth.

Jesus humbled Himself when He agreed to be the sacrifice for our sin. Leaving His place at God's right hand, the Crown Prince of heaven allowed Himself to be born into a human body that would ultimately be beaten and crucified to pay for our misdeeds. Jesus chose to humble Himself in order to carry out God's plan of salvation.

Humility doesn't require that you underrate yourself. Instead it encourages you to live with an appropriate understanding of who you are. Some say humility is a sign of weakness, but it's actually the hallmark of a healthy self-esteem. God had an amazing plan for Jesus' life, and He has a wonderful plan for your life as well. In order to accomplish it, you will need to embrace humility. It's more than a condition or an attitude; it's a choice.

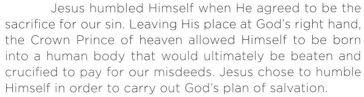

Dear Father,

I bow my knees before You,

the great Giver of Life.

Drain pride from my heart.

In its place, I choose humility.

I can do this because I know I'm Your child,

and I know You have a wonderful plan for my life.

Amen.

God Knows...
You struggle with commitment
...and He cares.

COMMIT YOUR WAY TO THE LORD, TRUST ALSO IN HIM,
AND HE SHALL BRING IT TO PASS.
PSALM 37:5 NKJV

You're drifting, never able to pull all the pieces of your life together. Relationships don't last, and neither do jobs. You start things but rarely finish them. When it comes to commitment, you can't seem to get there.

Fear of commitment is a serious problem, depriving you of love, fulfillment, even happiness. There could be any number of reasons why. Maybe you placed your trust in someone or something and got burned. Now you feel that making a commitment leaves you open to being hurt again. Whatever the case, the cure for what ails you has a name—Jesus.

Jesus made an all-in, definitive commitment to you when He gave His life. He has never failed you, and He never will. Commit yourself to Him in return, and you'll find that He's given you the power of His Holy Spirit to keep you strong and constant. Soon a positive cycle will be established. Each commitment honored opens the door to another, and another. Commitments should be carefully considered and entered into wisely, but once you've taken your stand, healing will come—with blessing right on its heels.

Dear Father,

I won't pretend I'm not afraid.

Nevertheless, I'm stepping forward,

committing to love You and follow You.

Thank You for Your unwavering commitment

that blesses and inspires me.

Amen.

Everything about us
is bare and
wide open to
the all-seeing eyes
of our living God.

HEBREWS 4:13 TLB

God Knows...
You've been betrayed
...and He cares.

**I AM STILL FULL OF CONFIDENCE,
BECAUSE I KNOW WHOM I HAVE TRUSTED.**
2 TIMOTHY 1:12 GNT

You might still be in shock, unable to accept that you gave your trust to someone, but got back nothing less than betrayal. How could a person you thought of as a friend have done this to you?

While you may never be able to figure out why it happened, let healing begin today. First and most important, allow God's Spirit to move your heart to forgive the betrayer. Anything less than forgiveness leaves an open wound that could destroy your ability to trust anyone. Next, ask God to help you examine what went wrong and draw from the devastating experience valuable lessons you can take with you into future relationships. Finally, refuse to let this incident define who you are or take away your sense of self-worth.

God cares about you, and that's something you never have to doubt. He's on your side, and at your side. God is faithful—always.

Dear God, grant me the ability
to forgive my betrayer,
because I know it's the only way to heal.
Help me move beyond this painful incident
so that I can open my heart
to trust again.
Amen.

God Knows...
You want to be a giver
...and He cares.

**YOU WILL BE ENRICHED IN EVERY WAY
FOR YOUR GREAT GENEROSITY.**
2 CORINTHIANS 9:11 NRSV

The Scriptures tell us it's more blessed to give than to receive. When you state your desire to be a giver, you acknowledge that you believe this assessment and agree that God rewards a generous heart. However, some people have turned this principle on its head by teaching that we should "give to get." In this case, giving is motivated by greed. Being a giver requires a pure heart, one unaffected by praise and ulterior motives.

The motivation behind your giving is important if you want it to have eternal value. All giving carries a reward, but giving in the way God intended has earthly as well as eternal rewards. Giving freely from a generous heart makes you more like Christ, who gave Himself without reservation. God's kind of giving will guard you against selfishness and greed, while establishing attitudes of kindness, compassion, love, and joy.

Desiring to be a giver is a great ambition—one you are not apt to regret. And remember, giving embraces more than monetary gifts. It includes your time, your energy, your expertise, your wisdom, and even your prayers. God loves the true-hearted giver.

Dear God,

I want to give to others

because You have given to me.

Of course, I will never be able

to pay You back fully,

but I want to give as much as I can

because You have given so much to me.

Teach me to be a wise

and compassionate giver.

Amen.

God Knows...
You're in need of perseverance
...and He cares.

TRIBULATION PRODUCES PERSEVERANCE;
AND PERSEVERANCE, CHARACTER;
AND CHARACTER, HOPE.
ROMANS 5:3-4 NKJV

As babies, we enter the world demanding instant relief from any discomfort. Parents must constantly tell their children to "wait," "hold on," and "be patient." But by the time we reach adulthood, most of us understand that the valuable and enduring things in life seldom come without delay, hard work, and perseverance.

For example, an education takes years of consistent study. Mastering a profession requires long hours and much effort for an extended period of time. Then there's marriage and raising a family—probably the most daunting long-term commitment of all.

Knowing that good things take time doesn't necessarily mean you always like the waiting and persevering—like children, we are all anxious and impatient at times. We put those feelings aside, however, because one day we realize that waiting is good for us. It teaches us to control ourselves, subjugate our will to God's will, and quiet ourselves enough to receive God's comfort and solace. God knows that waiting is uncomfortable and rubs your human nature the wrong way, but in the end, it will serve you well, helping you become a person of character.

Dear Father God,
thank You for teaching me
the benefits of waiting.
Even though it feels uncomfortable,
I know it builds character in my life
and helps me become the person
You created me to be.

Amen.

God Knows...
You're driven to achieve
...and He cares.

LORD; EVERYTHING THAT WE ACHIEVE
IS THE RESULT OF WHAT YOU DO.
ISAIAH 26:12 GNT

Money, possessions, accomplishments, advanced degrees, prestige—all these factors contribute to our society's overemphasis on achievement. In the material world, these make sense, but what happens when we look at them from a wider, spiritual viewpoint?

Human beings have difficulty seeing past the constraints of this life. God, however, espouses an eternal perspective. In spiritual and eternal terms, living in the center of God's will is the highest achievement of all. That doesn't mean we should abandon material success, but we do come to see that it lacks permanence.

If you feel yourself being driven to achieve in a world where results mean everything, ask God to raise your vision to include an eternal perspective. That could mean allowing God to use your achievements in ways you hadn't previously considered. It might even mean putting them aside in favor of fulfilling God's true and perfect will for your life. If you're ready to stop running after material success, ask God to raise your vision to include a spiritual perspective. You are certain to find that life is more beautiful and rewarding than ever.

Father, I'm tired of running after
one achievement after another
and never feeling like it's enough.
Help me direct my efforts
in ways that bring satisfaction and joy.
Amen.

God Knows...
You feel starved for love and affection
...and He cares.

HE BROUGHT ME TO THE BANQUETING HOUSE,
AND HIS BANNER OVER ME WAS LOVE.
SONG OF SOLOMON 2:4 NKJV

If you feel there's a deficit of love in your life, you aren't alone. When it comes to this greatest of human needs, a worldwide famine is raging. Parents abandon their children to selfishly indulge in drugs and alcohol, children rebel against their parents and take advantage of their elders, husbands and wives wage war, and friends come and go. Where can anyone find deep and satisfying love?

The Scriptures say God is the essence, fulfillment, and source of love. His love is strong and resilient, forgiving and boundless. No matter how many come to Him, there is more than enough for all. God's love is truly a feast in the wilderness. Best of all, God's love is a gift. All He asks is that you allow Him to fill your heart to overflowing so you can share His bounty with others.

Human love can never fully satisfy the love-starved heart. Only when it's mingled with God's love can it stand the test of time. God wants to love you like you've never been loved before, and He has invited you to His banquet table. Will you come?

Father God, thank You for love
that is more than enough
to satisfy my hungry heart.
Your love strengthens and heals me.
It makes me long to share it with others.
Thank You for welcoming me at Your table.
Amen.

God Knows...
You wonder if your life has purpose
...and He cares.

GOD IS ALWAYS AT WORK FOR THE GOOD OF EVERYONE WHO LOVES HIM. THEY ARE THE ONES GOD HAS CHOSEN FOR HIS PURPOSE.
ROMANS 8:28 CEV

Rare indeed is the person who hasn't asked, "Why am I here?" At one time or another, we've all wondered if our lives have purpose and what that purpose might be. Are our lives merely the result of a happy biological accident, or did God create each of us with a specific intention in mind?

You may be a lifelong God follower or relatively new to the life of faith. Either way, you may still be pondering the question of God's plan for your life. If that's the case, don't become discouraged. Rather than a sudden epiphany, most people grow into their God-destiny. Over time, the pieces fall into place.

Begin your journey of enlightenment by embracing God as your Creator and life as His gift. From there it's just a process of daily living and learning. God expects that there will be questions along the way. He doesn't mind. God knows you'll probably wander off the path from time to time. He's always there to show you the way back. God recognizes your persistence. So don't waste another minute wondering. Live your life one day and one discovery at a time.

Dear Father God,
thank You for giving me the gift of life.
I want to follow You
and discover daily the wonder of living
as You intended.
In this way, everything I do
will have meaning.
Amen.

God Knows...
You need courage
...and He cares.

BE STRONG AND COURAGEOUS,
ALL YOU WHO PUT YOUR HOPE IN THE LORD.
PSALM 31:24 HCSB

The soldier who risks his life to rescue a wounded comrade under enemy fire. The cancer survivor who goes through a long and uncomfortable treatment regimen without a complaint. The youngster who grows into a mature, stable adult despite negligent parents. It's tempting to think that people like these possess some sort of inner strength that the rest of us don't have. If we were to ask any one of them, however, they might say: "I'm not a hero. I simply did what I had to do."

While your courage may never be tested by extraordinary circumstances, your courage is routinely tested in ordinary situations. It takes courage to face daily frustrations with patience and humor. It takes courage to make good choices, such as doing for others even when it's inconvenient for you, or denying yourself pleasure now for the sake of your security or well-being later. In short, doing what you have to do every day takes courage!

When your courage wanes, remember that God is your place of rest. He sees and knows what it's like for you. He is your source of plain, everyday courage.

Dear Father,
give me the courage I need
to face each new day.
I often get bogged down
by my circumstances and limitations,
but I know I can stand strong
as long as I keep my eyes fixed on You.
Amen.

God Knows...
You blame Him for your circumstances
...and He cares.

It's pretty typical to blame God when things go wrong. Tsunami in Thailand—God. Famine in Africa—God. Blizzard in Albany—God. Our insurance policies even call disasters like these acts of God. It's human nature to take credit for the good and push off the bad on some force greater than ourselves.

The reality is that bad things happen to people—good people, bad people, all people. Sometimes those bad things are the result of our unwise choices, and sometimes they are the result of someone else's. In the beginning, God endowed humankind with freedom of choice and a perfect world. What happened next was our doing.

Blaming God for your misfortunes, while trendy, is tantamount to blaming the EMT who patches you up after the accident or the fireman who carries you out of the flames. God's intentions toward you are always good. Your peace comes in knowing that He grieves with you when things go bad, and He's always nearby, ready to offer His comfort and consolation. He's not one to point the finger and say, "I told you so!" Instead He promises His unconditional love and grace.

Heavenly Father,

You are great and mighty,

and it was You

who set in place the heavens and the earth.

And yet, You gave me freedom

to make my own choices.

Thank You for being there for me

when I need You and loving me through it all.

Amen.

God Knows...
You believe He's deaf to your prayers
...and He cares.

HE WILL ANSWER THE PRAYERS OF THE NEEDY;
HE WILL NOT REJECT THEIR PRAYERS.
PSALM 102:17 NCV

Time was when God seemed near, everything You said to Him brought a rush of emotion. But things are different now. Your prayers bounce off the walls, and His presence seems far away. What's going on? Has God abandoned you?

Most God-followers have experienced this discomfiting aloofness for a number of reasons. For example, sin is like a rip current. You wander out a safe distance only to find that you can't get back, no matter how hard you swim. Stop struggling, put yourself in God's hands, and He will get you back to shore. It could also be that you're talking too much and listening too little. In this case, God withdraws until you finally get all talked out. Or God may be teaching you to trust Him even when you can't hear Him or feel His presence—an important test of spiritual maturity.

Whatever the case, God cares. He has promised never to abandon you, and He always keeps His promises. Ask Him to replace your panic with peace. Then wait expectantly. He's closer than you think.

Holy Father,

You seem so far away,

but I believe that You will never abandon me.

Open my eyes to see why I feel this way.

I confess any sin in my life.

I promise to stop talking

and listen for Your voice.

And I thank You for testing my faith.

Amen.

God even knows
how many hairs
you have on your head.
Don't be afraid.
You are worth
much more than
many sparrows.

LUKE 12:7 NCV

God Knows...
You have a broken heart
...and He cares.

THE LORD IS NEAR THE BROKENHEARTED;
HE SAVES THOSE CRUSHED IN SPIRIT.
PSALM 34:18 HCSB

The mere thought of it once filled your heart with sunshine, but today the light and warmth is gone. Hopes and expectations are now marked by a wistful sigh at what could have been.

Your broken heart is a testimony to your deep and caring love, your energy and passion for life. Yours is a great heart and a vibrant spirit! Yet now your heart needs comfort and consolation. You are mourning the loss of your fondest hope and most cherished dream. So in the hands of your imagination, take each part of what you thought would be your reality and gently release it into the heavens. Will a tear go along with it? Yes, probably so. What you had every reason to think would take place, now won't.

As you lift your hands to the sky, take God's hands—He's reaching down to you! Let Him lift you up again. His caring and comfort heals. It's balm for a heart that will dare to hope and dream again!

Dear Father God, my heart is broken.

Right now, I can't imagine

how this is all going to turn out,

but I know that You

have a good future planned for me.

Grant me renewed hope

as I look to You.

Amen.

God Knows...
You don't sense His presence
...and He cares.

IN YOUR PRESENCE IS FULLNESS OF JOY;
IN YOUR RIGHT HAND THERE ARE PLEASURES FOREVER.
PSALM 16:11 NASB

They married young. After years of life together, their relationship changed from dreamy early love to tried-and-tested, mature love. Experience taught them that no matter what happened, they were there for each other. Emotions ebbed and flowed, but trust remained. For each, the presence of the other was never in question.

Your relationship with God may follow a similar pattern. Initially, you may be swept away by starry-eyed ideas of what God's presence feels like in your life. But with time those emotional highs seemed to dwindle. Does that make Him any less present? Certainly not! All it means is that your love for Him is maturing. You've come to realize that He'll be there for you not only when everything's going great, but when things are tedious or difficult or hard to bear—not only when you're feeling His presence but when you're wondering if He's there at all.

God's presence in your life is like the presence of someone who loves you day after day, year after year, season after season, because He does. He has pledged to you His constant presence, and He will keep His promise no matter what.

Dear Father God,

even when I can't feel Your presence,

I know You are here with me.

I will trust Your promises more than my feelings.

Thank You for knowing me so well

and reassuring me when I call out to You.

Amen.

God Knows...
You need wisdom
...and He cares.

FILL MY MIND WITH YOUR WISDOM.
PSALM 51:6 GNT

You're seeking wisdom, and that's a very good thing. It means that no matter how confused and uncertain you may feel right now, you deeply desire to do what is right. The Bible says that God is eager to answer the person who asks for wisdom. The question is, are you ready to hear Him?

Begin your quest for wisdom by seeking out the wise voices in your immediate world—parents, teachers, counselors, pastors—those people you've come to trust because of their wise choices in life. Listen to what they have to say. Then spend time in God's Word and prayer—quiet, ears-open prayer. Now that you've prepared your heart to hear God's voice, go about your daily routines. There isn't any formula for how God will unveil His wisdom to you, but you can be certain He will. At some point, you will just know what you're supposed to do.

Over time, you will learn that keeping company with wise people and keeping your heart prepared will serve you well. Wisdom will come to rest in your heart, easily accessible whenever you need it.

Lord God, more than anything else,

I want to do what is right.

Thank You for giving me the wisdom

I need to make right choices.

I will prepare my heart to hear

and act as You lead me.

Amen.

God Knows...
You desire to put Him first
...and He cares.

SEEK FIRST GOD'S KINGDOM AND WHAT GOD WANTS.
MATTHEW 6:33 NCV

You've been going through an old trunk that's been stored for decades in the attic of your family home. Inside you come across a packet of yellowed pages filled with your great-grandmother's tiny, neat handwriting.

What you discover surprises you. Born into a farm family, she learned how to work hard at an early age, but work didn't come first in her life. She was married with children, but her young family didn't come first, either. When a failing economy forced the family to move to the city, neither her losses nor her hardships came first with her. By the time you turn over the last page, you realize that your great-grandmother had always put God first. First in her thoughts, first in her budget, first in her plans.

God knows you want to put Him first in your life. That means you put Him first in all that life brings you, giving precedence to His instructions in the Bible and His whispers to your heart above your own thoughts and opinions. It means living your life as He directs. He asks this because He cares. He knows doing so will result in your best possible life.

Dear Lord,
thank You for showing me
that putting You first
does not mean giving away my life
but embracing my best possible life.
Show me how to follow You
wherever You lead.
Amen.

God Knows...
You fear the future
...and He cares.

YOU, LORD, ARE ALL I HAVE, AND YOU GIVE ME
ALL I NEED; MY FUTURE IS IN YOUR HANDS.
PSALM 16:5 GNT

Your fear of the future may be the result of realizing you have no control over it. None of us do. That's God's domain, not ours. But a change of perspective might help you overcome your fear.

Imagine that a blind man takes the arm of a seeing companion who leads him to a prescribed destination. The blind man must trust his seeing guide to lead him around obstacles and away from danger, and to keep him on the proper path. In the same way, we take God's arm as we make our journey through life. We can't see what comes next, but He does. As we follow His lead, He helps us navigate our way to our agreed destination.

Can you take God's arm and trust Him to lead you successfully through your life? Even if you say yes, this will take practice. Fortify your decision by acknowledging in your thoughts and speech that tomorrow belongs to God. There will still be walls, obstacles, and dangers, but keeping your hand on His arm will guarantee that you will successfully arrive at your destination. In time, you will lose your fear of the future, knowing that you can trust God unconditionally.

Dear Lord God,

I am taking a first step toward

overcoming my fear of the future.

I am taking Your arm and asking You

to guide me successfully through my life.

I believe that You will never abandon me

and nothing can separate me from Your love.

Amen.

God Knows...
You're in physical pain
...and He cares.

I AM SUFFERING AND IN PAIN. RESCUE ME,
O GOD, BY YOUR SAVING POWER.
PSALM 69:29 NLT

Physical pain can be all-consuming, a whole-body and mind experience. Add to that the harsh reality that no one can feel your pain but you. It is easily one of the most isolating, helpless feelings a person can experience.

You may be in that place right now. Medical intervention has failed, and your family and friends have given you all the comfort and sympathy they have to give—and yet, you continue to suffer. If you haven't done so already, it may be time to ask God for help. What can God do? you wonder. First of all, He experienced unimaginable pain on the cross, so He absolutely understands what you're going through. How He will relieve your suffering is a personal thing between the two of you.

God created our bodies to work perfectly. He grieves with us when the vulgarities of our flawed world cause them to break down. He may answer your prayer by supernaturally reversing your physical condition or by providing His wisdom and comfort and presence through it all. Either way, you will never again bear your painful burden alone.

Dear Lord, I'm hurting so badly.

I've looked everywhere for relief,

but nothing has helped.

I ask You to rescue me.

I place my body in Your hands

and ask you to do what You feel is best.

I trust You, Lord.

Amen.

God Knows...
You need a miracle
...and He cares.

HE ALONE PERFORMS GREAT MIRACLES;
HIS LOVE IS ETERNAL.
PSALM 136:4 GNT

Who doesn't say at times, "It's going to take a miracle to straighten out this mess." We talk about miracles, but we don't expect to see them. Our words simply mean the situation is dire, if not hopeless. If we are depending on natural means, such skepticism is warranted. But when God arrives, everything changes.

Don't let anyone tell you that God is no longer a miracle worker. He performed miracles throughout the Bible. No place do we read that He has retired His miracle-working power. Does that mean we're guaranteed a miracle? Let's think about that. God is our heavenly Father. He deals with each of us individually, and He's invited us to bring our requests directly to Him. He has also promised to answer us. But His answer might be yes, no, or even wait.

No matter what God chooses to do, He will make a way for you. It may not be the miracle you asked for, but He knows, in every situation, what is best. Remember that even when the answer is no, it shouldn't be viewed as an indictment but rather the answer of a loving father to the child He loves.

Heavenly Father,

I need a miracle, and I believe You

are still a miracle-working God.

Consider my request,

and give me the grace to accept Your answer.

Thank You for caring about me.

Amen.

God Knows...
You need emotional healing
...and He cares.

THE ONE WHO EXAMINES THE THOUGHTS
AND EMOTIONS IS A RIGHTEOUS GOD.
PSALM 7:9 HCSB

Our emotions are a wonderful gift from God. Without them we would be robots. With them, we have the ability to express an enormous range of feeling, both positive and negative. The problem comes when we begin to be immersed in negative emotion. This might be caused by a traumatic incident in our lives, a chemical imbalance, reaction to a medication, or one of many other reasons. Our emotional make-up is a highly complex operating system.

Unfortunately, emotional wounds cannot be seen. Unlike a gash in your arm or leg that draws a gasp from others, emotional wounds go largely unnoticed until the sufferer decides to share his pain with someone else.

When you experience emotional pain, it's tempting to suffer in silence. Don't do it. Share your wounded thoughts and emotions with someone you trust. Love and understanding are good medicine. At the same time, it's important to share your pain with God. Unlike anyone else in your life, He is able to see your pain and already knows its source. He wants to give you a big dose of His healing power. Reach out to Him and He will surely reach back.

Precious Lord, I need You
like I've never needed anyone before.
Give me the courage to share my pain
with someone who can help me
through this difficult time,
and I ask You to expose and heal
the source of my suffering.
Amen.

God Knows...
You've experienced disappointment
...and He cares.

Disappointment can shake your confidence and cause you to question everything—even God. But God loves you, and He has promised never to disappoint you. That is good to know when you consider that He's the only one who can make such a promise. Everyone else in your life will disappoint you at some point. It's what humans do. You've probably even disappointed yourself at times.

Discussing the "hows" and "whos" of your disappointment aren't nearly as important as asking yourself, *What's next?* Will you let God help you recover and get back on your feet? Focusing on a negative experience only serves to cheat you out of fresh experiences with new people, places, and things. Instead, hang onto what you've learned, pick yourself up, and get back to living your life.

God doesn't like to see you disappointed. That's why He goes out of His way to let you know He will never fail you. Take His hand, receive His wisdom, listen to your spiritual instincts, and take your time making choices. These simple steps will make you better able to skirt disappointment in the future.

Lord God, help me
put this disappointment behind me,
and keep my heart open
to new experiences.
I want to learn from this without
letting it trip me up.
Thank You for helping me
make a fresh start.
Amen.

God Knows...
You are struggling to respect yourself
...and He cares.

IF YOU PUFF YOURSELF UP, YOU'LL GET THE WIND KNOCKED OUT OF YOU. BUT IF YOU'RE CONTENT TO SIMPLY BE YOURSELF, YOUR LIFE WILL COUNT FOR PLENTY.
MATTHEW 23:11-12 THE MESSAGE

God knows how important it is for you to respect yourself. He doesn't want a sense of unworthiness to overshadow the blessings He sends your way. Nor does He want feelings of inadequacy to keep you from finding satisfaction in your abilities and accomplishments. When you fail to respect yourself, you are failing to respect Him—your creator.

Well-grounded self-respect begins with you believing that you are God's handiwork. He created you, and He doesn't create junk! Nothing about you or your circumstances can change the fact that you are wonderfully and marvelously made. Let this truth permeate your heart and mind. Stand in front of a mirror and say, "God created me, and I respect what God has made." Hold onto this thought as you go about your day. If there are things you normally think, do, and say that are not worthy of you, start making changes for the better. If there are people in your life who disrespect you, start firmly but gently standing up for yourself.

When you respect yourself, you're respecting someone God created, loves, and cares about. To Him, you are priceless.

Creator God, thank You
for seeing me—knowing that I need
to respect and stand strong for myself.
Grant me the strength and power
to claim the self-respect that is mine
because of Your great love for me
and my value in Your eyes.
Amen.

The Lord knows
what is in
everyone's mind.
He understands
everything you think.
If you go to him
for help, you will
get an answer.

1 CHRONICLES 28:9 NCV

God Knows...
You're in the grip of an addiction
...and He cares.

GOD IS A SAFE PLACE TO HIDE, READY TO HELP
WHEN WE NEED HIM. WE STAND FEARLESS AT THE
CLIFF-EDGE OF DOOM.
PSALM 46:1-2 THE MESSAGE

You may have been able to control it in the past, but now it controls you—your time, your thoughts and desires, your finances, your health. But be encouraged. Realizing you need help is the first step to reclaiming your freedom.

Jesus, who came to earth to model His Father's compassion for all who suffer, healed many of their physical, mental, and emotional distresses. Most important, He healed the worst addiction of all—sin and the guilt that comes with it. His healing work continues to this day. Let Him free you as you turn to Him with a humble, repentant heart. Your forgiveness is assured! Now ask Him to lead you away from the addiction. He may encourage you to change the way you spend your time and money, cultivate friends who will help you maintain a wholesome lifestyle, or discover new interests. He may also lead you to a medical professional, twelve-step program, even rehab. God knows you will need human helpers.

The first step to overcoming addiction is admitting you have a problem. You've done that. Now, take God's hand, and let Him lead you through the deep waters to freedom.

God of all strength,
walk with me on the road to recovery,
because I'm surrounded by pitfalls
and temptations.
Fill me with the power to persevere
no matter how long the journey.
Lead me to the freedom
I so desire.
Amen.

God Knows...
You've suffered an injustice
...and He cares.

HE GIVES JUSTICE TO ALL WHO ARE TREATED UNFAIRLY.
PSALM 103:6 TLB

God knows His children suffer injustice at the hands of others. He knows it's painful and frustrating when we realize we have no control over what others do. He has, however, given us the power to control how we respond.

Our natural desire is to lash out. Yet in trying to hurt those responsible as much as they have hurt us, we're prolonging and intensifying our own suffering. In His ministry, Jesus modeled a better way to face injustice. To hatred, insults, and rejection, He responded with love and compassion. To those who manipulated His trial, to those who scourged and mocked Him, and to those who nailed Him to the cross, He offered full and complete forgiveness. Unnatural? For us, definitely. But not for our God. He knew that God, His Father, would deal with their evil deeds.

Base your response on the firm foundation of God-empowered love, compassion, and forgiveness, essentially for your own sake. God does expect us to speak out against injustice of all kinds, but we are to do so with pure hearts, trusting Him to tip the scales and avenge the perpetrators in His own good time.

Heavenly Father, Jesus forgave
all those who persecuted Him.
Grant me the willingness, power,
and grace to speak out against injustice,
while retaining a heart of love,
compassion, and forgiveness.
Amen.

God Knows...
You're overwhelmed with guilt
...and He cares.

COME NEAR TO GOD WITH A SINCERE HEART AND A SURE FAITH, WITH HEARTS THAT HAVE BEEN PURIFIED FROM A GUILTY CONSCIENCE AND WITH BODIES WASHED WITH CLEAN WATER.
HEBREWS 10:22 GNT

It might not be something specific, or it might be. Either way, guilt has a way of simmering in the background. Though we imagine it's a whisper about an issue we can think about later, God hears it as a shout that needs to be dealt with now. And sooner or later, we will too. Guilt eventually boils over into all areas of life.

When your guilt gets too hot to ignore, give thanks! Your soul's anguish is your sure indication that God cares about you. You realize that guilt will persist until you do something about it. Sure, you could bury it under layers of excuses, but it would still be there in the depths of your soul. That's why God has provided you with guilt relief through His Son Jesus. He has taken on your guilt so you can live guilt-free, free to live with a light and joyful heart.

Like a whistling tea kettle, guilt is a call for attention. Let its whistle bring you to sincere repentance, because your forgiveness is a certainty. Let your repentant prayer leave you comforted and ready for the freedom He has for you.

Redeemer God,

You have done everything necessary

to take away my guilt.

I plead for Your forgiveness!

Cleanse me with a firm faith

in Your redeeming work,

and remind me daily that I am completely

guilt-free in Your sight.

Amen.

God Knows...
You desperately want a child
...and He cares.

"BREAK FORTH INTO JOYFUL SHOUTING AND REJOICE ... FOR THE [SPIRITUAL] SONS OF THE DESOLATE ONE WILL BE MORE NUMEROUS THAN THE SONS OF THE MARRIED WOMAN," SAYS THE LORD.

ISAIAH 54:1-2 AMP

God knows you're hurting. Even the sight of an infant in a stroller makes your heart sob, much less the tiny newborns that your friends so proudly cradle. Of course you smile. You congratulate. But you also hurt. You, too, would like a child to call your own. So why hasn't it happened?

Ultimately, the gift of children comes from the Creator of life—God. We cannot say why some women bear children so easily while others do not. But what we do know, because He has given us examples in His Word, is that He has blessed women with children even after the women themselves had given up hope. Also, He sometimes gives childless women special callings that have fulfilled them and blessed those around them for generations.

Allow your longing for a child to be a blessing as it draws you closer to Him. Rest your trust firmly in His wisdom as you discern His good will for your life. When you see a mother cradling her infant in her arms, remember that God holds you close to His heart. Let this image remind you of His enduring love.

Giver of Life,

You know the longings of my heart.

Help me accept and embrace

Your good will, no matter what it is,

because You alone know what is best

for today and for the future.

Amen.

God Knows...
Your life is complicated
...and He cares.

COME TO ME, ALL OF YOU WHO ARE WEARY AND BURDENED, AND I WILL GIVE YOU REST.
MATTHEW 11:28 HCSB

Everything's a mess! Problems are coming at you from so many directions that you just can't get your mind around a prayer. You've promised yourself that you'll get working on your relationship with God as soon as you get your life straightened out.

But guess what? The more complicated your life is, the more you need God's guidance. The harder it is to pray, the more you need prayer's power. Regardless of how perplexing, painful, frustrating, or confusing things are right now, God knows and cares. Even if you find it impossible to fully express yourself in prayer, rely on His Spirit to supply the words that you cannot. Perhaps this is the time He has chosen to bring you closer to Him as you receive His peace and comfort. Maybe now you're ready to receive deeper faith in His presence, stronger reliance on His strength, and heightened appreciation of how He works in your life.

Today, spend some quiet time with God. He cares about you, about what's going on, and about everyone involved. Give it all to Him and rest at ease.

Father God, You know
all about the issues I'm facing right now.
Please help me make the right choices,
because I don't know which way to turn.
Through it all, keep me close to
You and trusting in
Your strength and wisdom.
Amen.

God Knows...
You're consumed with fear
...and He cares.

I ASKED THE LORD FOR HELP,
AND HE SAVED ME FROM ALL MY FEARS.
PSALM 34:4 CEV

What will happen next? That's what sets your heart trembling and your mind whirling with worst-case scenarios. Before you know it, fear consumes your thoughts and fear warps every aspect of your life.

God-given fear turns you away from dangerous situations. It reminds you to be cautious before taking risks, and keeps you diligent when it comes to your safety and well-being. When fear becomes your overwhelming emotion, however, it throws off your perspective. All you can see is danger ahead! This is far from what God intends, and that's why He invites you to trust Him with every aspect of your life.

When fear threatens to take over, tell God what you're afraid of, even if you can't tell anyone else. Sit quietly in His presence as He clears away the fog of fear so you can begin thinking calmly, clearly, and rationally. Learn how to separate fact from fiction, present reality from inflammatory predictions. Let fear work for you, not against you.

Lord, You know all my fears.
Help me put my trust
completely in You
so that I am not prey to unrealistic
and distressing thoughts.
Turn each of my fears
to deeper reliance on You.
Amen.

God Knows...
You need His strength
...and He cares.

THE GOD OF ALL GRACE, WHO HAS CALLED YOU TO
HIS ETERNAL GLORY IN CHRIST, WILL HIMSELF RESTORE,
SUPPORT, STRENGTHEN, AND ESTABLISH YOU.
1 PETER 5:10 NRSV

You're just exhausted—maybe physically, but more intensely mentally and emotionally. Now you realize you've felt this way for quite a while and the circumstances of your life aren't likely to let up anytime soon.

When the needs and responsibilities of each day make you wonder how you're going to get through it, God invites you—urges you!—to come to Him for rest, soul-deep rest. But He's not going to send you back into the fray without providing some practical help—His strength. He will give you what you need to carry through with your God-given responsibilities and the wisdom to walk away from unproductive activities. Perhaps He will renew your sense of purpose by bringing to mind how your work blesses others. Or restore your energy by opening to you a fresh perspective. Or He might strengthen you by sending help from a source you never expected!

Things aren't easy right now, but God is ready to help. Ask Him for His strength. And during the day if you feel that old weariness coming on, ask Him for some more!

Father God, I need your strength
because I've used up the last drop of mine!
Take me in Your loving arms,
and grant me the rest
of heart and mind that I need
to fully embrace today and the days ahead.
Amen.

God Knows...
You don't like getting older
...and He cares.

THE RIGHTEOUS WILL FLOURISH LIKE PALM TREES; ... THAT STILL
BEAR FRUIT IN OLD AGE AND ARE ALWAYS GREEN AND STRONG.
PSALM 92:12-14 GNT

Remember when you couldn't wait to reach, say, your teen years? Your twenty-first birthday? Then you celebrated your big 3-0 and started wishing time would slow down a little!

God knows getting older isn't comfortable, but it's part of life—the life He's given you. Why not celebrate what the years have brought you, rather than focus on what they have taken away? Your life experience has shaped you into the unique person you are today, equipping you to take God's plan for you to a higher level. Perhaps He even has a new direction for you, one you could never have managed before! After all, the years have allowed you to come to terms with who you are, your strong points and shortcomings alike, and you're comfortable in your own skin. And you've learned that life is short. You're more careful to cherish your loved ones and more eager to make memories than gather possessions. You know what really matters to you.

God has blessed you with something not everyone gets the privilege of reaching—the age you are today. Give Him thanks for the past, and praise Him for the future He has in store for you.

Dear heavenly Father,
thank You for the years You have given me
and all the blessings they have brought.
Fill me with the joy of living,
and keep me ever young at heart.
Amen.

God Knows...
You're living as a single
...and He cares.

THE TIME AND ENERGY THAT MARRIED PEOPLE SPEND ON CARING
FOR AND NURTURING EACH OTHER, THE UNMARRIED CAN SPEND
IN BECOMING WHOLE AND HOLY INSTRUMENTS OF GOD.
1 CORINTHIANS 7:33 THE MESSAGE

You may have chosen to go solo, or that may be simply where you find yourself. Either way, God makes it clear that He blesses the single life. The Bible provides many examples of single men and women who have led purposeful, productive, remarkable, and rewarding lives.

The Bible also points out that the single life allows you to have a rich God-life with fewer distractions. It's likely that you have more time than your partnered friends to sit with God, reflect on His teachings, and learn from Him. You're probably freer to follow your interests and passions as well, and to be God's hands and feet in the lives of others. If you have been single for a while, you know how to be alone but not lonely. You're comfortable being your own person.

No matter what anyone else says, being single for life is completely consistent with God's will and purpose. And even if one day you decide to change your status to married, God knew all along and has already written it into the plan. God only asks that you embrace the life you have and live it to the fullest.

Dear God, grant me the perception
and the power to live
a God-pleasing life as a single person.
Help me through its special challenges,
and keep me always attentive
to the things I can do to honor
You and serve others.

Amen.

God Knows...
You're dealing with a difficult person
...and He cares.

WE WHO ARE STRONG HAVE AN OBLIGATION TO BEAR
THE WEAKNESSES OF THOSE WITHOUT STRENGTH.
ROMANS 15:1 HCSB

Sometimes they're in the workplace as associates, customers, or clients. They could be neighbors, fellow church members, or even someone in your family. Difficult people come into your life, and you can't always simply walk away from them!

While it's easy to focus on the burden they are to you, imagine what burden they must be to themselves. What internal issues torment them? What experiences have so warped their perception that they see the world in such a negative light? Perhaps more than any others, these difficult people in your life need your prayers. And as you speak to God about them, ask Him for the wisdom to respond in the kindest and most helpful way. Think of a more productive way of dealing with the words and actions that prevent good relationships. Or imagine yourself engaging each of them in a private conversation in which you share your concerns and listen to theirs.

Most of all, practice patience. Your consistent understanding, kindness, and compassion will not only help you keep your cool, but over time, you also might see some positive changes in your most negative relationships!

Heavenly Father,

there are people in my life

who are very difficult to get along with.

More than anyone else,

You know why they act this way.

Use me to help make a difference for the better,

because You dearly love all of us.

Amen.

God Knows...
You need answers
...and He cares.

You're smart to take your medical questions to your physician, not to Dr. Anonymous on the Internet and your money questions to your financial advisor, not to a neighbor who's perpetually in debt. When you take your spiritual questions to God, you're going to the best place you can go for answers!

The Bible declares that God created you and loves you. He clearly reveals His plan of eternal salvation for you as a believer in the life, death, and resurrection of His Son Jesus. That He desires a personal relationship with you is evident in His Word—He calls you friend, invites you to speak to Him freely, and promises to send His Spirit to enliven and enlighten your heart. Other questions? Many answers can be discovered as you delve further into Scripture, because some passages serve to clarify others. Trained theologians and religious scholars offer their insights on difficult or complex questions. Their work is often arranged by subject for easy reference.

Still curious? Maybe you have one of those questions that God chooses not to answer—and that's okay. You can trust Him with a good mystery!

Dear Father God,
through the work of Your Spirit
in my heart, help me believe what You teach,
even when it goes against popular thought.
You are Creator, Redeemer,
Life-Giver—the One who really knows!
Amen.

God Knows...
You have a disability
...and He cares.

Why it is, we don't know, but people often fear anything that is different from what they understand and know, such as people and cultures from other countries and people who don't look or speak like they do. Then consciously or unconsciously they often deal with their fear by lashing out. It's possible that you've experienced this firsthand. In addition to the physical and mental hardships created by your disability, you may have been the target of bullying or ridicule or simply ignored.

God knows that being different has been painful for you, and He cares. After all, Jesus was different too, and He was subjected to harsh ridicule and mockery by those who feared His popularity with the people and His power to heal. You won't be able to change how other people see you, but you can keep things in perspective by remembering that God created you, not some idealized version of you, but you.

God shaped you and formed you with His own hands, and He's proud of His work. You are not a mistake. He loves you, and He has promised to walk by your side through every second of every hour of every day.

Dear God,

the fact that I'm different

does create obstacles and hardships for me.

I'm glad that You understand,

and I'm so glad You have promised

to walk with me through my life.

Amen.

God Knows...
You have a problem with anger
...and He cares.

HE WHO IS SLOW TO ANGER IS BETTER THAN THE MIGHTY,
AND HE WHO RULES HIS SPIRIT THAN HE WHO TAKES A CITY.
PROVERBS 16:32 NKJV

They say you have a short fuse. And in your heart of hearts, you have to admit that it's true. It doesn't take much before the red-hot flame of anger shoots up within you to the point where you can't do anything else except explode!

Anger, like any other God-given emotion, can serve us well, or destroy our relationships and well-being. Productive anger, that is, anger that works for the good, is controlled anger directed at evils such as cruelty, murder, injustice, and terrorism. It leads us to actively seek solutions in whatever way lies within our power. Destructive anger, however, lashes out uncontrollably at whatever or whoever happens to be its target. It solves nothing and produces only destruction.

Ask God not to remove anger from you but to help you get it under control. An anger-management counselor can give you some practical suggestions to get you started. God cares about your struggle with anger. He wants to help you find positive ways to cope when you feel anger welling up within you. Discover how you can use your emotions, your passion, even your anger to make a difference for good.

Father God, I beg your forgiveness
for the damage my anger has done.
I want to change.
Enable me to learn new ways
to deal with and control my anger
so I can use it in a productive
and God-pleasing way.
Amen.

God Knows...
You struggle with worry
...and He cares.

DON'T WORRY ABOUT ANYTHING;
INSTEAD, PRAY ABOUT EVERYTHING.
PHILIPPIANS 4:6 NLT

You just can't help worrying! And there's no lack of things to worry about, is there? God knows the thoughts that keep coming at you, the worries that whirl around in your head all day, and the anxiety that keeps you up at night. They are strong, pervasive, and persistent. But God isn't just giving you a pat on the head when He says, "Don't worry." Instead, He teaches you how not to worry.

First, God urges you to pray about everything that agonizes you—big or small. If it's a concern to you, it's a concern to Him. He wants you to pull it right out of your head and give it to Him, and then leave it with Him! Second, He invites you to remember all the things you've worried about in the past that didn't happen. He was taking care of you then, just as He is now and will in the future. Third, He asks you to trust and rely on Him because He cares about you, and that's not going to change.

When God says, "Don't worry," take Him at His word. Allow yourself the joy and peace of a worry-free day—and night.

Dear God, free me
from the habit of constant worry.
When worries threaten me,
remind me that You are there for me
to trust and rely on.
Grant me the peace of heart and mind
that I can only find in You.
Amen.

God Knows...
You want to be married
...and He cares.

YOUR CREATOR WILL BE YOUR HUSBAND;
THE LORD OF HEAVEN'S ARMIES IS HIS NAME!
ISAIAH 54:5 NLT

Most adults want to be married. They yearn to have someone special in their lives, someone who will care for them and about them, someone to love, support their dreams, and cherish the memories they make together. But so far, you haven't met that special person.

You may have asked God many times—maybe for years—to send the right person into your life. Though He understands your impatience, His will and His timing reach far beyond human comprehension. Put your trust in His plans for you, whatever they may be, because they will work out for your good. Besides, the Lord has promised to serve as your husband for as long as you need Him. But while you wait, don't wait to live. Take the opportunity to grow spiritually, to read, study, and learn. Embrace your interests. Develop skills and expertise in an area that attracts you.

Pray for the special person you will meet in God's good time, if marriage is His will for you. Ask Him to open your eyes to see beyond superficial appearances, because so often true love is found when and where it's least expected.

Lord God, grant me
the gifts of patience and acceptance,
because You know how eager I am
to receive the blessing of marriage.
Keep me faithful to the life
You would have me live,
and walk with me on the path
You have set out for me.
Amen.

God Knows...
You long for peace
...and He cares.

**YOU WILL EXPERIENCE GOD'S PEACE,
WHICH EXCEEDS ANYTHING WE CAN UNDERSTAND.**
PHILIPPIANS 4:7 NLT

A glance at the headlines tells you that the world is not a peaceful place. A few minutes of listening to others reveals that very few hearts and minds are truly at peace. A look into your soul exposes inner restlessness and discomfort, despite the fact that Jesus came to earth as the Prince of Peace.

Fortunately, the peace that Jesus brings does not depend on outer circumstances or inner feelings. If it did, His peace would be unattainable to those living, say, in a war zone or a troubled household, and unavailable to anyone suffering under an emotional burden. The peace God gives is a deeper peace, an enduring peace, and one that can see you through any upheaval the world has to offer. He knows what you're dealing with. That's why He's provided the only peace that can keep you steady in heart and mind, despite the turmoil around you. His peace alone will stay at the core of your being, calming and quieting your emotions.

Don't wait for the world or your life to get peaceful before you find peace. Let God's Spirit fill your heart with the peace that is yours in Jesus!

Lord Jesus, Prince of Peace,
fill me with the kind of peace that lasts.
When trouble is all around
and anxiety simmers within,
grant me the blessing of soul-deep hope,
faith, and peace.
Amen.

LIVE YOUR FAITH

Dear Friend,

This book was prayerfully crafted with you, the reader, in mind—every word, every sentence, every page—was thoughtfully written, designed, and packaged to encourage you...right where you are this very moment. At DaySpring, our vision is to see every person experience the life-changing message of God's love. So, as we worked through rough drafts, design changes, edits and details, we prayed for you to deeply experience His unfailing love, indescribable peace, and pure joy. It is our sincere hope that through these Truth-filled pages your heart will be blessed, knowing that God cares about you—your desires and disappointments, your challenges and dreams.

He knows. He cares. He loves you unconditionally.

BLESSINGS!
THE DAYSPRING BOOK TEAM

Additional copies of this book and other DaySpring titles can be purchased at fine bookstores everywhere. Order online at dayspring.com or by phone at 1-877-751-4347